That Was
The Church
That Was

That Was The Church That Was

Cartoons by Marty Murphy

A Nostalgic Quiz
for Indulgent Catholics
Edited by Joel Wells

THE THOMAS MORE PRESS
Chicago, Illinois

ISBN 0-88347-158-2

CONTENTS:

"Dear Editor: You need take no pride,
'humble' or otherwise, in your cartoons.
They are...revolting...crude...vulgar...
not in accord with Vatican II...pornographic
...not fit to go through the U.S. mail...
nauseating...sordid cesspool material...
and by a Murphy, no less! **Et tu Brute?**"

Introduction

The "That-Was-the-Church-that-Was" Quiz at the back of this book is the work of many nostalgic hands. The cartoons are the work of one quick but steady hand—Marty Murphy's. All appeared in *The Critic* magazine (R.I.P.) in the late 60s and early 70s when the American church was in the throes of change and upheaval which seemed all too deadly serious to many people—so much so that *The Critic,* with the help of Marty Murphy and several other talented cartoonists, sought, brashly perhaps, to lighten up the scene. The work of the "other" *Critic* cartoonists was sampled in an earlier book—*Pilgrim's Regress* (now out of print) but Marty Murphy proved so prolific that he deserves a private showing for the new generation of the 80s. Here, in his own words is his life in a nutshell:

"I'm a very immature 50 years old. I got started drawing cartoons of nuns and priests while in the 3rd grade of St. Michael's School, Wheaton, Illinois.

"I got out of the army in 1956 and went to work in the Hollywood animation industry. Shortly thereafter I also started selling magazine gags. For the last eight years I've been writing stories and designing characters for an animated film series co-produced in Europe and Japan.

"I currently live in an old house in the middle of Los Angeles with my wife, three dogs, four or five cats, and a wolf at the door."

5

ONE
NUN
AND
THE
MODERN
WORLD

"Sister! Sweetie! Baby!"

"Anything in our rule that says I can't
give this meathead a piece of my mind?"

"Now THAT I like!"

"Quick, grab a baseball and some bats!
Here comes a photographer."

"A penny for your thoughts, Sister."

"I'm sure Sister will understand
that Hollings is rather special."

"Let's go in and see if we can
Christian them down a little."

"This will be our little secret, huh Timmy?"

"If it wasn't for me you wouldn't be
able to write at all, Johnny Burke."

"What's the matter, Sister, haven't you ever been whistled at before?"

"Well, you just 'naturally assumed' wrong!
We'd like some brochures on Las Vegas!"

CASUALTIES
OF
RENEWAL

"Today, a long-awaited announcement
from the Vatican!"

"They never did figure out what went wrong."

"I'm sorry ladies, but smoking
is still one of our little no-no's here."

"My kid says he wants to become a priest
but I keep tellin' him: 'Get into
something more permanent...'"

"Because those clowns at the Ecumenical Council said the Jews didn't kill Christ; **that's** why all of a sudden we gotta forgive the Jews for killin' Christ!"

"I don't get it! It walks, it talks, it glows
in the dark. So why don't it sell?"

"Hi everybody! Welcome to another edition
of the good old 9:15. This is Ed, 5th-Sunday-
after-Pentecost, Cavanaugh, your friendly
commentator, talkin'..."

"...and I ate meat on Friday, and I didn't
fast during Lent, and I went to see a 'B' movie...
and I..."

A.C.

What life may be like in the future, "After Celibacy."

"Now don't start giving me that
'good-old-days' routine again."

"...but really, the very first time I saw Ed
saying the 12:15 Mass, I said to myself,
'that's the man for me!'"

"Oh sweetheart!...I have a little confession to make."

"Oh! It's your **niece** is it, Monsignor Reilly.
Saints preserve us! For a moment there I thought
that **you**...that is that **she**...that is
the two of you had..."

39

"Oh! Honestly daddy and mommy,
you're really so old-fashioned!"

"I wish just for once you wouldn't compare
my chicken soup with the soup your
housekeeper used to make."

That Was The Church That Was

"Now my advice to you would be to bury your pride
and try to see her side of it. Remember,
the Lord said, 'Blessed are the...'"

42

"And then darling, we could honeymoon at the Vatican
or maybe Lourdes...or even the Holy Land."

"And do you...you...you renegade...
take this girl to be..."

"Oh yeah! Well you ain't exactly
no Barry Fitzgerald yourself!"

"How did I first meet your mother?
Well, kids, that's a long, long story."

"Would you mind knocking off that 'My Son' stuff. . .
After all, you **are** my dad."

MARTY MURPHY
previews that fateful day when

ST. AGNES
OF THE WOODS
GOES CO-ED

"Well Sister, the rumors must be true!"

"It's from St. Agnes College! Now why the
hell would I want to enroll at a girl's school?"

"That's not exactly
what I had in mind."

"That's not exactly
what I had in mind."

"Now wait just a darned minute here!"

"Yes dear, I realize you come from a large family --
seven brothers and four sisters. I understand.
But here at St. Agnes we..."

"What's my major?
Oh, I'm studying for the priesthood."

"We've been checking your transcript Mr. Mulroy,
and not only were you **not** a seminarian at
St. Ambrose College, but you're not even a Catholic.
Just what is your little game?"

"It's not what we thought, Sister!
She's just giving haircuts."

"A word with you, Mr. Entrepreneur."

"No use stalling any longer. Let's
go make our first (gulp) bed check."

"And remember the time back in '61 when we caught Gladys
Fenwich with a bottle of gin in her foot locker.
And she was suspended for a whole semester. And remember
the time Edna Gerd missed Sunday night curfew?"

"Pop, I've decided where I want to go to college...
St. Agnes of the Woods!"

ONE
HOLY
CATHOLIC
AND
WHITE

"Those little rascals sure do like to dress up, don't they."

"Ah hah! I thought so!"

"Bless you my son! Bless you my son!
Bless you my boy! Bless you my son!"

"They'll change the water, won't they?"

"This is our new church!"

"This is our power plant!"

3

"This is our new school!"

4

"...And this is our negro!"

"That's a Southern Methodist?"

"Oh my God! Guess who's coming to dinner?"

THE POPULAR ELECTION OF BISHOPS

OF BISHOPS

Will Politics Bring Out the Beast in Priests?

"And I'm getting pretty tired
of your holier than thou attitude!"

"Do you notice anything different around here?
Or is it just me?"

"Yes sir, we're both quite aware what marriage and a family could do to my political career."

"You've become like one of the family over the years, Mrs. Cassidy. I hope that during these last few weeks of my campaign, we can count on you to keep your big mouth shut!"

"You can sure tell it's an election year."

"Never mind what your sainted mother would
think; just worry about what the Catholic League
of Women's Voters is going to think."

"And while you're saying that ridiculously short penance you could be walking down Third Street handing out these flyers."

"While we're all gathered here together, let's not forget that a vote for me is a vote for integrity, leadership and a return to a more meaningful way of worship."

"I think we've found the skeleton in Father Dubinsky's closet. Seems as if a second cousin on his mother's side was a FALLEN AWAY CATHOLIC!"

"He'll not get my vote -- looks too Jewish!"

"You won't find me conducting a mud-slinging
campaign like my opponent, who, by the way,
just happens to be a convert."

✝ shirts

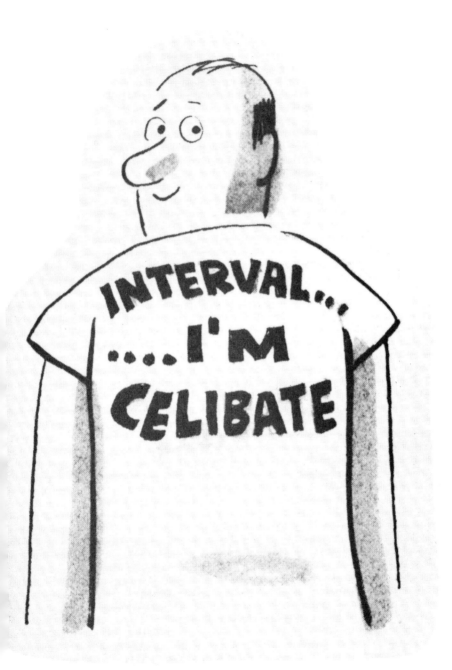

BRING BACK
ST. CHRISTOPHER

When Women
Become Priests

brother Foley?
Mary Alice Foley S.J.
The Rev. Mary Alice Foley
THE RT. REV MARY ALICE FOLEY
Father Foley??
Bishop Foley
MSGR. Foley!
Mary Cardinal Foley
her holiness, Mary I
O.K. WOMEN FOR PRIESTHOOD

"So **you're** the new assistant. I sure as hell
don't know what all the fuss is about."

"Remember, it is God's will...it is God's
will... it is **God's** will...it is...."

"Now she's changing the missal to the Gospel side...No, wait a minute...Now she's putting it back... Now she's re-arranging the flowers ...Now she's moving the candels in closer...Now she's picking up the missal again...No! Now she's...

"Well, how'd your first afternoon in the box go?"

"For heaven's sake, all I said was I
wondered how I'd look in a hat like that!"

"But aside from the vow of poverty
how does the rectory differ from the convent?"

"I'm sorry my children, but I always cry at weddings."

"A priest's life would not be an easy one for you, my child. What can **you** know about golf? Or fund-raising? Have you ever raffled off a Cadillac? Do you...."

"I really don't know if the gold with the white piping looks better on you than the purple. I **do** know that on the seventh Sunday after Pentecost we wear green, period!"

"...A note under my door. Either you go or she goes."

"That crazy girl who entered the priesthood.
What does she want now?"

"Women priests! Good Lord! What next?"

"Dad, I think I have a vocation.
Dad, I want to become a nun!"

"Bernie, it's a natural! Priests meets nun...
priest **loves** nun...priest loses nun!"

The times they're
still a' changin'...

"It's his First Communion picture!
Won't he at least take off his 'shades' for that?"

"Remember . . . we tell them we're **priests** . . .
That **always** works."

"I can't give you any Do's and Don'ts
about birth control, young lady. Only Don'ts."

"You mean he wants to go to confession . . . RIGHT NOW?"

"It's not a sacrilege, Agnes! I need something
to wedge between the carburetor float and the throttle
linkage. Now give me the dashboard statue."

"Just a simple gesture is sufficient when
we make the sign of peace, Mr. Fenwick.
No more passing out business cards. O.K.?"

"Joe here is a marketing consultant specializing in motivational research. He's going to run a little film entitled 'Making the Most of That Second Collection.'"

"Frankly, I'm worried, Sister.
Attendance at **this** mass is dropping off, too."

"No kidding? **The Moon Is Blue** . . . .
I excommunicated a guy for watching that back in '52."

"Bless us, Father . . . Our last confession was . . ."

How many things are wrong
with this drawing?

1. Henry VIII Circular window.
2. No corpus on crucifix.
3. Candles not lit.
4. Mary and Joseph Altars on wrong side; Joseph wearing bib-overalls.
5. Tabernacle door is open and missal is on wrong side.
6. Altar not facing people.
7. Woman celebrant and altar girls.
8. Pray is misspelled in sign.
9. Side windows are open admitting fresh air *before* anyone has fainted.
10. Usher sneaking smoke.
11. Too many Stations.
12. Raffle tickets are priced too low.
13. Dog in church.
14. Man throwing coins into holy water font.
15. Charge for church parking (though this may not be far off).
16. Lock on vigil-light offering box has not been jimmied.
17. Women playing bingo in pews.
18. Families are too large; none of the babies are crying.
19. Child coming out of confessional has not reached the age of reason.
20. Priest giving sermon is on the wrong side and is missing canonical digits.
21. Altar and Rosary society women are sitting in Holy Name Society pews.
22. When did you ever go to confession to a priest named Goldburg?
23. One usher is taking up collection during sermon and another is smiling at late arrivals.
24. Congregation at right is kneeling during sermon.
25. Nuns are kicking in to the collection.
26. Boy selling newspapers in center aisle.
27. Only pew left with seats is occupied by two old ladies who are *not* blocking either end.
28. Bongo player is wearing hat.
29. Teenage girls entering church are not wearing jeans.

That-Was-the-Church-that-Was
QUIZ

SOMEWHAT arbitrarily, the QUIZ that follows is divided into two parts: VENIAL and MORTAL. The VENIAL questions are, by-and-large, easier than the MORTAL. And within these categories questions have been assigned a weighted score in an ascending order of difficulty. Correct answers to questions in the VENIAL category will bring scores of from 1-4 points each whereas those in the MORTAL section bring rewards of from 5-8 points. The compilers will not presume to say what a really good or terribly poor score might be. They suggest that you simply score yourself honestly, or have your answers verified by a friend in case you are the sort of person inclined to give yourself the very broad benefit of any doubt. For comparison at the level of the universal Church it may be helpful to know that Pope John Paul I missed 36 questions total in both parts, but then he did not have the advantages of an American parochial school education.

While it is difficult to assign a hard and fast cut-off date, the questions and answers and much of the terminology of the QUIZ are definitely associated with the pre-conciliar Church—that is before the Second Vatican Council (or Pandora's Box II as it is referred to by our more conservative brethren). Subsequent reforms and revisions are not taken into account. QUIZ-takers must bear this in mind.

The compilers are well aware that some of the language in the questions and answers is sexist, or has strong sexist overtones—but then so was the pre-conciliar Church (and, some say, so is the post-conciliar Church). Females who truly wish to enter into the spirit of the QUIZ will thus wear a hat, mantilla or other suitable headcovering (not a handkerchief) and will not don short-sleeved dresses, shorts or other immodest attire. No one wearing jeans should take the QUIZ and males over 16 (though it is doubtful that anyone under this age could begin to compete) are expected to wear a jacket and tie.

While it can't be guaranteed, an ejaculation to St. Thomas Aquinas has been known to raise scores appreciably.

That-Was-the-Church-that-Was
QUIZ

[Number following question indicates points earned by the correct answer, which can be found in the pages following Part II of the Quiz.]

Part I: *Venial*

1. To whom should you pray for recovery of lost articles? (1)

2. Name the Joyful Mysteries of the Rosary. (3)

3. Describe the Paten and its use. (3)

4. What is a mite box? (4)

5. Name two great "social encyclicals." (2)

6. What is the "seal of confession"? (1)

7. What prominent Hollywood actress wrote a regularly syndicated column for the Catholic Press? (4)

8. What is the *Baltimore Catechism*'s answer to the question "Why did God make me?" (1)

9. Name the Glorious Mysteries of the Rosary. (3)

10. What are the first six words of the Memorare? (1)

11. Name the magazine that was distributed at Novenas of the Sorrowful Mother. (4)

12. What is the correct written form of address for a Monsignor? (2)

13. What is the first line of the *Tantum Ergo?* (1)

14. Name the Sorrowful Mysteries of the Rosary. (3)

15. What is a prie-dieu? (2)

16. Who was the founder of the Jesuits? (1)

17. What does the acronym CYO stand for? (1)

18. Who founded the CYO? (4)

19. Did chewing gum break the Lenten or Eucharistic fasts? (3)

20. How many Holy Days of Obligation are there in the U.S.? What and when are they? (4)

21. What saint was roasted over a fire? (2)

22. Who was called "The Radio Priest"? (1)

23. What is a postulant? (3)

24. What is a scapular? (2)

25. Who wrote the novel *The Power and the Glory?* (4)

26. Who played the older priest in the movie *Going My Way?* (1)

27. Which of the Apostles was crucified upside down? (2)

28. Which hat does each of the following wear: Cardinal? Bishop? Priest? (3)

29. What is the next line of this song: "Oh Mary we crown thee with blossoms today . . ."? (3)

30. Who was known as the "Leper Priest" and where was his mission? (1)

31. What was the special intention of the "Leonine Prayers" prescribed by Leo XIII to be said at the conclusion of Mass? (4)

32. On what day is the feast of St. Joseph? (2)

33. In what three films did Bing Crosby play a leading role as a priest? (3)

34. In what country is the shrine of Our Lady of Fatima located? (1)

35. Name three of the four popes who were in office between the years 1900 and 1925. (4)

36. The Virgin Mary, identifying herself as the Immaculate Conception, appeared to a 14-year-old girl near the French town of Lourdes. What was the girl's full name? (2)

37. What are the Ten Commandments?—Thou shall not be imprecise! (4)

38. Where is the United States' National Shrine of the Immaculate Conception located? (1)

39. What Italian saint was murdered while defending her virtue? (1)

40. Name the Italian Capuchin monk reputed to bear the stigmata? (2)

41. What is the name of the Pope's summer residence? (3)

42. Name one book by Dr. Tom Dooley. (3)

43. Who was the Maid of Orleans? (1)

44. Who is the patron saint of Ireland? (1)

45. What are the five "liturgical colors"? (4)

46. Who wrote *The Imitation of Christ?* (2)

47. What are the two months of the year officially dedicated to Mary? (1)

48. The name of what other author is most often associated with G. K. Chesterton? (3)

49. What is the official newspaper of the Holy See? (3)

50. What is the month of the Poor Souls? (1)

51. Who is the patron saint of travelers? (1)

52. Who was the first martyr? (2)

53. Ashes distributed on Ash Wednesday come from what source? (1)

54. Give the names of three Archangels mentioned in the Bible. (4)

55. Who used to erase the blackboard on Bishop Sheen's television show? (3)

56. Properly attired altar boys wear what two items of dress? (2)

57. Where is the Golden Dome? (1)

58. Name four Notre Dame football coaches since Frank Leahy. (3)

59. Who painted the ceiling of the Sistine Chapel? (1)

60. What does the term "Black Pope" mean? (4)

61. On what two days of the year may a priest say three Masses? (2)

62. What is the Shroud of Turin? (1)

63. What was the family name of Pope Pius XII? (3)

64. What is a Perpetual Novena? (2)

65. The Blessed Mother appeared to St. Catherine Laboure and commissioned her to make a medal of the Immaculate Conception and spread devotion to Mary under this title. What is the name of the medal? (3)

66. What is Peter's Pence? (1)

67. Give the common or popular name for the (a) Order of Preachers and (b) the Order of Friars Minor. (3)

68. What is meant by the term "Devil's Advocate"? (4)

69. The blood of what saint is said to liquify from time to time? (3)

70. What is a "National Parish"? (2)

71. Name two of the personal missals widely used in this country. (1)

72. What is a catechumen? (3)

73. What does the St. Vincent DePaul Society do? (2)

74. Candles used on the altar at Mass must contain a proportion of what substance? (3)

75. What does it mean to be "churched"? (4)

76. When is Pentescost celebrated? (3)

77. What is a reliquary? (1)

78. What is "Viaticum"? (2)

79. Who are the four Evangelists? (1)

80. What is the Holy Office? (3)

81. Distinguish between a (a) Solemn High Mass and (b) Low Mass. (2)

82. Distinguish between a (a) plenary indulgence and (b) partial indulgence. (4)

83. What is the name of the prayer said daily at morning, noon, and evening as the church bell rings? (1)

84. What does the "Forty Hours Devotion" memorialize? (3)

85. Name at least six of the original Twelve Apostles. (2)

86. Was St. Ignatius, founder of the Jesuits, a sailor, soldier or carpenter? (3)

87. What does "ex cathedra" mean? (4)

88. Translate: *Ad majorem Dei gloriam.*

89. What is a Mass card? (1)

90. What is a "firm purpose of amendment"? (2)

91. What is the name given to an offering made to a priest with the understanding that he will say a Mass for a particular person or purpose? (1)

92. Who was the missionary saint to Indonesia who is also the patron of the foreign missions? (4)

93. Who was the "Happy Warrior"? (3)

94. On what day are the altars stripped? (2)

95. What are the three theological virtues? (3)

96. What are Ember Days? How often do they occur? (4)

97. Distinguish between the (a) Ordinary and (b) Proper of the Mass. (3)

98. Mass formerly ended with a reading from the introduction to the Gospel of St. John. What was this called? (1)

99. Name the three principle parts of the Mass. (2)

100. How many choirs of angels are there? Name at least four. (4)

101. Who is the patron saint of lawyers? (2)

102. Who co-starred with Bing Crosby in *The Bells of St. Mary's?* (1)

103. What is a first-class relic? (3)

104. What feast day was formerly celebrated on January 1st? (2)

105. What is the small gold container carried on a sick call by a priest called? (3)

106. What is the Laetare Medal? (4)

107. What is the sacred vessel in which the Host is displayed during Benediction called? (2)

108. During what liturgical times of the Church year are nuptial Masses forbidden? (3)

109. On whose feast day are throats blessed? (1)

110. Mass is celebrated every day of the year with what one exception? (2)

111. Hand bells are not used during Mass from Holy Thursday to Easter Vigil. What replaces them? (3)

112. Name the feast celebrated on December 28th to commemorate the children murdered by King Herod? (1)

113. What name is given to a special week-long series of talks and devotions aimed at the spiritual renewal of parishioners? (2)

114. Who was the first "Negro" saint?

115. On what night of the week are Novenas to the Sorrowful Mother held? (2)

116. What is considered the age of reason under Church law? (1)

117. How often must marriage banns be announced in order that the canonical requirements for valid announcement be met? (2)

118. What is an "Imprimatur"? (3)

119. On what particular day of Holy Week is the hymn *Pange Lingua* sung? (2)

That-Was-the-Church-that-Was
QUIZ

Part II: *Mortal*

120. Who is the "Saint of the Impossible"? (5)

121. What is "Sun Time" and how did it apply to the Eucharistic fast?" (7)

122. Who founded "The Christophers"? (6)

123. What is a quarantine? (8)

124. Distinguish between the Virgin Birth and the Immaculate Conception. (5)

125. What is hyperdulia? (8)

126. What are the first three lines of the *Dies Irae?* (7)

127. What is probably the only dogma infallibly proclaimed by the pope alone, rather than by a Council? (6)

128. Name six of the eight Beatitudes. (5)

129. What is the Hypostatic Union? (8)

130. What is a ferial day? (6)

131. What is the Pauline Privilege? (7)

132. Explain the origin of the name "papal bull" applied to a pontifical document. (8)

133. What is a Moveable Feast? (5)

134. Name three Moveable Feasts. (6)

135. What were the main provisions of the Lateran Treaty? (8)

136. Who wrote *Tom Playfair* and *Claude Lightfoot?* (5)

137. What was the name of the comic strip that ran on the last page of *Extension* magazine? (7)

138. How is the date for Easter determined? (8)

139. What is a *sacrarium?* (6)

140. What is exclaustration? (7)

141. At a funeral Mass for a priest, his feet (or the foot of the casket), are arranged differently from that of a casket containing the remains of a lay person. What is the difference? (8)

142. What is Laetare Sunday? (6)

143. The movie *The Prisoner* was about whom and what? (7)

144. Name three of the twelve fruits of the Holy Spirit. (6)

145. "Tantum Ergo, Sacramentum . . ." is the first line of a hymn. What is the next line? (5)

146. Name four of the seven gifts of the Holy Spirit. (8)

147. Name the four Cardinal Virtues. (7)

148. Name three of the six precepts of the Church. (8)

149. What does "O Salutaris Hostia" mean in English? (5)

150. What is an auto-da-fe? (6)

151. Give the name of the legendary "female pope." (7)

152. What is the difference between a Religious Order and a Congregation? (8)

153. Who were the APAs? (7)

154. What saint chased a harlot from his room with a burning faggot? (6)

155. Why did the Pope decree that if a suspected heretic was being questioned by a Dominican, a Franciscan had to be present? (8)

156. What is the name of the small container which holds the incense to be placed in the censer? (5)

157. What are two definitions of "pall"? (7)

158. What are the names of the three children of Fatima? (6)

159. What saint was so corpulent that the table had to be cut away so that he could get close enough to his food to eat it? (8)

160. What is the Portiuncula Indulgence and how is it obtained? (7)

161. Who played Bernadette in the 1944 film, *The Song of Bernadette?* (5)

162. What two novels by Alexander Dumas are listed on the Index of Forbidden Books? (7)

163. Who was the third century martyr who was killed while carrying Communion to Christians in prison? (8)

164. Name the American Jesuit theologian and ecumenist who was an international expert on Church-State relations. (6)

165. What does "ad limina" refer to? How frequent must "ad limina" visits be? (8)

166. Name two North American martyrs. (5)

167. Who was the Arctic Priest? (7)

168. Of the 29 officially acknowledged "Doctors of the Church" only two are women. Name them. (6)

169. What is the highest award/honor a Catholic Girl Scout can receive? (8)

170. What does discalced mean? (5)

171. What Pope resigned to become a hermit? (7)

172. What Pope is known as "the Pope of the Eucharist"? (6)

173. Describe a wimple. (7)

174. The devotion known as "Nine Fridays"—going to Mass and receiving Communion on nine successive "First Fridays" of the month—resulted from a promise purportedly made to what saint? (5)

175. What are Rogation Days? (8)

176. What is the *Ratio Studiorum?* (6)

177. Who wrote *Introduction to the Devout Life?* (5)

178. What was the name of the Curé of Ars? (7)

179. What are canonical digits? (8)

180. Who was the first American bishop? (5)

181. An offering given on the occasion of the performance of certain sacraments is called what? (7)

182. Name two foreign Catholic authors popular in the U.S. who won the Nobel Prize for Literature. (6)

183. Until recently, what Catholic fraternal organization refused membership to bartenders? (5)

184. A newly created Cardinal whose name the Pope keeps secret is said to be a "Cardinal in _____." (7)

185. What saint, especially popular with Italians, is often depicted with a dog? (6)

186. What saint—one of the original twelve Apostles—was martyred on a cross in the form of the letter X? (5)

187. What name is given to the sin defined as having "the expressed will of buying or selling something spiritual"? (8)

188. Who was Bishop Noll? (6)

189. Who was Cardinal Gibbons? (5)

190. Name five of the seven capital sins. (7)

191. Who was Georges Rouault? (5)

192. What is the *Asperges?* (6)

193. At what time of day is the Compline section of the Divine Office read? (5)

194. Which saint, when responding to a petition, always sends "a thorn with the rose"? (8)

195. Who was chosen to take the place of the traitor Judas? (6)

196. In what country is the Patna Mission located? (5)

197. Altar candles are always lit in what proscribed sequence? (7)

198. Name the Roman emperor who not only became a Christian but required all of his subjects to do the same. (6)

199. What is the Black Fast? (5)

200. What was the Oxford Movement? (6)

That-Was-the-Church-that-Was
QUIZ ANSWERS

[Number in parentheses indicates number of points earned by the correct answer.]

Part One—Venial

1. St. Anthony (of Padua). (1)

2. The Annunciation, The Visitation (of Mary to Elizabeth), The Birth of Jesus (Nativity), The Presentation (of Jesus in the Temple), The Finding of Jesus in the Temple. (3).

3. A flat, circular gold plate which holds the Host to be consecrated during the Mass. (2)

4. A small box distributed to churches during Lent to collect contributions made for the missions. (4)

5. *Rerum Novarum* and *Quadragesimo Anno*. (2)

6. The obligation upon the confessor not to reveal the matter confessed nor the identity of the one confessing. (1)

7. Loretta Young. (4)

8. "God made me to know Him, love Him, and to serve Him in this world and to be happy with Him forever in the next." (1)

151

9. The Resurrection, The Ascension, The Descent of the Holy Spirit, The Assumption, The Crowning of Mary (Coronation). (3)

10. "Remember O most gracious Virgin Mary . . ." (1)

11. *Novena Notes.* (4)

12. Very, or Right Reverend. (2)

13. "Tantum Ergo Sacramentum." (1)

14. The Agony in the Garden, The Scourging at the Pillar, The Crowning with Thorns, Carrying of the Cross, Christ's Death on the Cross. (3)

15. A kneeler for prayer. (2)

16. St. Ignatius of Loyola. (1)

17. Catholic Youth Organization. (1)

18. Bishop Bernard Sheil. (4)

19. Yes, as it exhibited a lack of respect and was a violation of the spirit rather than the letter of the law. (3)

20. Six: Christmas, Dec. 25th; Circumcision, Jan. 1 (now called Solemnity of Mary the Mother of God), Ascension, 40 days after Easter, Assumption, Aug. 15, All Saints, Nov. 1, Immaculate Conception, Dec. 8. (4)

21. St. Laurence. (2)

22. Charles Edward Coughlin. (1)

23. A candidate for admission into a religious order. (3)

24. (a) Two small pieces of cloth connected with strings, worn on the chest and back under the clothes as a token of a particular devotion; (b) a sleeveless outer garment falling from the shoulders, often worn as part of a religious habit (Dominicans, for example.) (2)

152

25. Graham Greene. (4)

26. Barry Fitzgerald. (1)

27. Saint Peter. (2)

28. Cardinal—red hat; Bishop—mitre; Priest—biretta. (3)

29. "Queen of the angels, Queen of the May." (3)

30. Father Damien de Veuster; Molakai. (1)

31. For the conversion of Russia. (4)

32. March 19th. (2)

33. *Going My Way; The Bells of St. Mary's; Say One for Me.* (3)

34. Portugal. (1)

35. Leo XIII; Pius X; Benedict XV; Pius XI. (4)

36. Bernadette Soubirous. (2)

37. 1. I, the Lord, am your God. You shall not have other gods beside me.
    2. You shall not take the name of the Lord, your God, in vain.
    3. Remember to keep holy the Sabbath day.
    4. Honor your father and your mother.
    5. You shall not kill.
    6. You shall not commit adultery.
    7. You shall not steal.
    8. You shall not bear false witness against your neighbor.
    9. You shall not covet your neighbor's wife.
    10. You shall not covet anything that belongs to your neighbor. (4)

38. Washington, D.C. (1)

153

39. Maria Goretti. (1)

40. Padre Pio. (2)

41. Castel Gandolfo. (3)

42. *Deliver Us from Evil*
The Night They Burned the Mountain
The Edge of Tomorrow. (3)

43. Saint Joan of Arc. (1)

44. Saint Patrick. (1)

45. White, red, green, purple, black. (4)

46. Thomas a'Kempis. (2)

47. May and October. (1)

48. Hilaire Belloc. (3)

49. *L'Osservatore Romano.* (3)

50. November. (1)

51. Saint Christopher. (1)

52. Saint Stephen. (2)

53. Palms left over from the previous year's Palm Sunday distribution. (1)

54. Michael, Raphael, Gabriel. (4)

55. His angel. (3)

56. Cassock and surplice. (2)

57. Atop the administration building of the University of Notre Dame, South Bend, Indiana. (1)

58. Terry Brennan, Joe Kuharich, Ara Parseghian, Dan Devine, Gerry Faust. (3)

59. Michelangelo. (1)

60. The Superior General of the Jesuits. (4)

61. All Souls' Day and Christmas. (He can always binate, and can say three or more Masses, according to the needs of the people, with the bishop's consent.) (2)

62. It is thought by many to be the burial shroud of Jesus. (1)

63. Eugenio Maria Giuseppe *Pacelli*. (3)

64. A devotion that goes on indefinitely, even after the customary cycle of nine observances. (2)

65. Miraculous Medal. (3)

66. Annual world-wide collection in support of the Holy See. (1)

67. (a) Dominicans; (b) Franciscans. (3)

68. The official who carefully examines the life, work, miracles, etc. of a candidate for canonization or beatification. (4)

69. Saint Januarius. (3)

70. A parish that is limited to membership of a specific nationality group rather than by its geographic boundaries. (2)

71. St. Joseph's; St. Andrew's; Father Stedman's; Marian; Maryknoll. (1)

72. One under instruction in the faith awaiting baptism. (3)

73. An international society of Catholic laymen who serve as volunteers and perform works of charity for the poor. (2)

74. Beeswax—51 percent. (3)

75. Blessing given to women in church after childbirth. (4)

76. Fifty days after Easter. (3)

77. A container or box, often with a transparent lid, made to hold a relic of a saint. (1)

78. Communion given to a dying person or one in danger of death. (2)

79. Matthew, Mark, Luke and John. (1)

80. Doctrine of the Faith Congregation. It is the highest ranking department of the Roman Curia. (3)

81. (a) Sung Mass with a deacon and subdeacon and six candles; (b) Recited, not sung, no deacons, two candles. (2)

82. (a) Remission of all temporal punishment due to sin; (b) remission of part of the punishment due to sin. (4)

83. Angelus. (1)

84. Christ's forty days in the desert or wilderness. (3)

85. Simon Peter; James; John; Andrew; Philip; Bartholomew; Matthew; Thomas; James Alphaeus (the Lessor); Jude Thaddeus; Simon the Canaanean; Judas Iscariot. (2)

86. A soldier. (3)

87. Literally "from the chair"; it refers to infallible papal pronouncements in matters of faith and morals. (4)

88. "To the greater glory of God." (3)

89. A card stating that Mass will be offered for a particular person or intention, giving the name of the donor. (1)

90. Sincere intention to sin no more, and firm resolve not only to avoid sin but to avoid as far as possible the near occasions of sin. (3)

91. Stipend. (1)

92. Francis Xavier. (4)

93. Al Smith, the first Catholic to run for President. (3)

94. Holy Thursday. (2)

95. Faith, Hope, Charity. (3)

96. Three days each quarter for special penance and prayer—Wednesday, Friday, Saturday—fasting and partial abstinence from meat. (4)

97. (a) Ordinary is relatively unchangeable; (b) Proper changes from day to day. (3)

98. The Last Gospel. (1)

99. Offertory, Consecration, Communion; following Mass of the Catechumens. (2)

100. Nine: Seraphim; Cherubim; Thrones; Dominations; Principalities; Powers; Virtues; Archangels; Angels. (4)

101. Thomas More. (2)

102. Ingrid Bergman. (1)

103. First class relics include the skin and bones, clothing, objects used for penance, instruments of a martyr's imprisonment or passion. (3)

104. The Circumcision. (2)

105. A pyx. (3)

106. Annual award to an outstanding Catholic made by the University of Notre Dame. (4)

107. Monstrance. (2)

108. Lent, Advent, Sundays and Christmas. (3)

109. Saint Blaise. (1)

110. Good Friday. (2)

111. Wooden clappers. (3)

112. Holy Innocents. (1)

113. Parish Mission. (2)

114. Peter Claver. (4)

115. Friday. (2)

116. Seven. (1)

117. Three successive Sundays. (2)

118. The name of the ecclesiastical approval required for publication of all books, pamphlets, etc., that insures they are free from error in matters of faith and morals. (3)

119. Holy Thursday.

Part Two—*Mortal*

120. St. Jude (5)

121. A person had to make a consistent choice about fasting according to a diocese. One could not eat until midnight in a diocese which followed Sun Time and then go across the border into another diocese which followed Standard Time and eat until midnight there, as well—and then go back and receive Communion in the Sun Time diocese. (7)

122. Rev. James Keller (2)

123. A period of forty days—frequently associated with indulgences.

124. The Virgin Birth signifies Mary's constant virginity through Christ's conception and birth; The Immaculate Conception relates to the fact that Mary herself was conceived without Original sin. (5)

125. The special veneration accorded to the Virgin Mary, as distinguished from adoration or worship, which is properly accorded only to God. (8)

126. Dies irae, dies illa
    Solvet saeclum in favilla
    Teste David cum Sibylla. (7)

127. The dogma of the Assumption of Mary. (6)

159

128. Blest are the poor in spirit; the reign of God is theirs.
Blest are the sorrowing; they shall be consoled.
Blest are the lowly; they shall inherit the land.
Blest are they who hunger and thirst after holiness;
they shall have their fill.
Blest are they who show mercy; mercy shall be theirs.
Blest are the single-hearted; for they shall see God.
Blest are the peacemakers; they shall be called sons of
God.
Blest are they persecuted for holiness' sake'
the reign of God is theirs.   (5)

129. The union of human and divine natures in the one
divine person of Christ. (8)

130. A weekday on which no proper feast is celebrated in
the Mass or Liturgy of the Hours (Divine Office). (6)

131. The exception under which a legitimate marriage,
even one consummated, of unbaptized persons can be
dissolved in favor of one of them who subsequently
receives the sacrament of baptism. (7)

132. The decree is sealed with a lead disk called a "bulla."
(8)

133. One that is not celebrated on the same calendar day
each year. (5)

134. Easter; Pentecost; Trinity Sunday; Ascension; Christ
the King. (6)

135. Vatican City is an independent state; Catholicism is
the official religion of Italy; the Holy See relinquished
title to former Papal States. (8)

136. Father Finn. (5)

137. Little Davy. (7)

138. The first Sunday after the first full moon following the vernal equinox. (8)

139. A basin with a drain leading directly into the ground (standard in sacristies). (6)

140. Permission for a religious to live outside his or her religious house but to retain the obligation of vows and affiliation with the community. The right to obedience is tranferred from the religious superior to the local ordinary (bishop) where the exclaustrated religious resides. (7)

141. Priest's feet point toward the altar; lay persons' point toward the congregation. (8)

142. The fourth Sunday of Lent. (6)

143. Hungarian Cardinal Mindzenty's resistance against the Communist takeover of his country. (7)

144. Charity; Joy; Peace; Patience; Benignity; Goodness; Longnanimity; Mildness; Faith; Modesty; Continence; Chastity. (6)

145. "Veneremur cernui . . ." (5)

146. Wisdom; Understanding; Knowledge; Counsel; Piety; Fortitude; Fear of the Lord. (8)

147. Prudence; Justice; Fortitude; Temperance. (7)

148. (1) Keep the Sundays and Holydays of Obligation by assisting at Mass and desisting from servile work.
    (2) Fast and abstain on the days appointed by the Church.
    (3) Go to confession once a year if serious sin is involved.
    (4) Receive the Blessed Sacrament during the Easter season.

161

(5) Contribute to the support of the Church and its pastors.

(6) Do not marry within certain degrees of kindred nor solemnize marriage during a forbidden time. (8)

149. "O Saving Victim"—the traditional Benediction hymn. (5)

150. The public announcement and execution of the sentence of the Inquisition—broadly, the burning of a heretic. (6)

151. Pope Joan. (7)

152. A Religious Order is an institute whose members profess solemn vows; a Congregation is an institute whose members profess simple vows. (8)

153. American Protective Association—Revived the anti-Catholic issue in the U.S.; declined after 1896. (7)

154. Thomas Aquinas. (6)

155. During the Spanish Inquisition, in order to temper the Dominican's propensity to cruelty. (8)

156. The boat. (5)

157. (a) A black cloth placed over a casket; (b) A cardboard covered with cloth used to cover the chalice. (7)

158. Lucy (Lucia), Jacinta and Francisco. (6)

159. Thomas Aquinas. (8)

160. Sometimes called "the Pardon of Assisi"; a plenary indulgence originally attached to the small chapel within the Bascilica of St. Mary of the Angels in Assisi, Italy, for August 2; since 1924 it may be

gained as often as the conditions are fulfilled; since 1939 any pastor may, with his bishop's permission, apply to the Sacred Penitentiary for the privilege of having the Portiuncula Indulgence in his parish. (7)

161. Jennifer Jones. (5)

162. *The Three Musketeers; The Count of Monte Cristo.* (7)

163. St. Tarcisius. (8)

164. John Courtney Murray. (6)

165. Refers to the quinquennial reports bishops are required to make to the Vatican. Bishops of continents other than Europe must make the visit every ten years but their reports must be submitted every five years. (8)

166. Antony Daniel; Charles Garnier; Gabriel Lalemant; Isaac Jogues; John de Brebeuf; John Lalande; Noel Chabenel; Rene Goupil. (5)

167. Father Hubbard. (7)

168. Catherine of Sienna and Teresa of Avila. (6)

169. Marian Award. (8)

170. Without shoes—barefoot. (5)

171. Saint Celestine V (1215-1296), who was Pope from August 29, 1294 to December 13, 1294. (7)

172. Pius X. (6)

173. A cloth covering for the head and neck, formerly worn by many women religious. (7)

174. Saint Margaret Mary Alacoque. (5)

175. The Monday, Tuesday and Wednesday before Ascension Thursday; celebrated for the purpose of obtaining a good harvest. (8)

176. The abbreviated term for the Jesuit curricular and methods guide, which appeared in 1599 under the title *Ratio Atique Institutio Studiorum Socieatis Jesu.* (6)

177. Francis de Sales. (5)

178. Jean-Baptiste Vianney. (7)

179. The thumb and index finger of each hand of a priest, consecrated by a bishop at ordination. (8)

180. John Carroll. (5)

181. A stole fee. (7)

182. Sigrid Undset; François Mauriac. (6)

183. Knights of Columbus. (5)

184. "Petto." (7)

185. Saint Rock. (6)

186. Saint Andrew. (5)

187. Simony. (8)

188. (1875–1956) Ordinary of the Diocese of Fort Wayne, Indiana; in 1912 he began to publish *Our Sunday Visitor.* One of the founders of the Catholic Press Association. (6)

189. Considered the greatest ecclesiastic in American Church history (1834–1921); ordained in 1861, consecrated bishop in 1877; wrote *The Faith of Our Fathers,* 1876, the most successful work of its kind in the apologetical literature of American Catholicism. (5)

190. Pride; Covetousness; Envy; Anger; Lust; Gluttony; Sloth. (7)

191. French impressionist artist; the suffering and passion of Christ were frequent subjects. (5)

192. Rite of sprinkling the faithful with holy water before High Mass on Sundays. (6)

193. At the end of the day—the last service of the day, an evening prayer. (5)

194. St. Rita of Casica. (8)

195. Matthias. (6)

196. India. (5)

197. Begin with candles nearest crucifix (center) on Epistle side of altar, proceeding outward (left to right); next on Gospel side, but from right to left. (7)

198. Constantine. (6)

199. A self-imposed Good Friday fast which prohibits intake of all dairy products in addition to meat. (5)

200. A movement initiated by Anglican clergymen at Oxford University (1833–45) to renew the Church of England by revival of some Roman Catholic doctrine and liturgy. John Henry Newman, the movement's leader, made his profession of Catholic faith in 1845 and was later created a Cardinal. (6)